Tattoos of Him

Tattoos of Him

Memoir of a Domestic Abuse Survivor

By Christine Matotek

For all the survivors and victims of domestic violence. May they come to peace with the tattoo of the abuse their personal badge of courage that they should never be ashamed to share.

ACKNOWLEDGEMENTS

This book is dedicated to God and my wonderful family (my mom and dad, brothers, Michael, Andrew aka Prophet Andrew, Joseph and my sister, Angela and Ines, Jacqueline, Shianne and Amalia, who are both wise beyond their years, and Uncle Fred & Aunt Earla, and Kathryn) who continued to love me unconditionally even when I didn't love myself; or, believe I was loveable. I love you all! A huge hug to my friends Tara & Elizabeth for all their unconditional support and love. I would also like to thank all the therapist, doctors, nurses, EMT, police officers, firemen, professors and neighbors that have helped me over the years. And a very special thank you to Women in Distress for all their help and wonderful resources.

CAUSE

Writing this cause

My paper and pen

Seem to understand

They don't accuse me

Or tell me how

I should feel

Silently they sit

Waiting for me

To expel the words

I hold within

Patiently my pen

Holds my hand

As I let go

Of my inner demons

One letter at time

Maybe this poem

Will be the one to

Free them forever

Table of Contents

CHAPTER 1

Dreams are made
Of perfect diamonds
On your finger
And white picket fences

It was all so perfect
How he surprised me
I thought it was a dream
He took me
To Washington, DC

He looked sharp in his tux
I had my princess black gown on
Ready for a night
On the town
When he said
Let's stop and see
The Lincoln Memorial

I wondered why
He would want
To go to a place
That was being restored
But he loved history
And politics
So why not

As we stopped

In front of Lincoln
I wondered how
It felt to be free

When you knew
Nothing but bondage
All your life
A life lived in fear
Then one day
You were told
To walk away
You were free
Would you know
How to live
Would you be scared
How would you
Figure out how
To make decisions
On your own

My mind drifted
Away from my thoughts
Of slavery
As I saw him
Acting sort of weird
He looked uncomfortable

All of a sudden
He bent down
On the wide steps
It looked like he
Had to scratch
His ankle
But then down
On one knee he went
Would you marry me

The little black box
Held a diamond ring
All I had to do
Was say yes

The sparkle seemed
To dance around me
Gleefully I thought about
How he chose me
He wanted me to marry him
Of course
I said yes
I will marry you

He slipped the golden ring
On my finger
Holding my hand out
I admired the diamond
That glistened in the moon light
That diamond
Sealed the deal
He was going
To be my lifelong mate

For a split second
I thought this is not
What I should do
Runaway
Don't stay
He's up to his controlling ways
Manipulating me

Oh but I wanted
To be wanted
To have a diamond

To smile
And say yes
This is my fiancé
So that moment passed

I ignored myself
Shut up
I told my mind
You'll ruin the dream
Just be quiet
Maybe he'll change
For now just enjoy
Your time
As your finger sparkles
In the moonlight
On the stairs
Of the president
Who set the slaves free

Don't think of
Last week's black eye
Or your bruised arm
It's no reason to be alarmed
For can't you see
He wants nothing else
But for you to be happy

CHAPTER 2

No more ring
Ringing in my ears
As the tears
Have flowed too much
Over the past years
The many fears
I must deal with
Steer me on my journey
As I switch gears
Realizing the many dears
That have been
On my path
But none so near
As the one
I fear

CHAPTER 3

As he stepped into the room
She felt it
The adrenaline rush
Thrashing through her
As he got closer
And closer
The air became thicker
For every molecule
In her body
Seemed to be overcome
By his presence
Memories flooded her
His fist coming right at her face
Yes he had a permanent place
In her head
Even though she tried
To get rid the memories
They always came back
Surrounding her
Making her surrender to the pain
Of yesterday as if it were today
They even swirled
Around her fingertips
As if to say
Her identity would
Never be her own
For he would forever own her

CHAPTER 4

Don't peel the layers
Back too far
You might get
A glimpse of
The real me
It's something
I don't want
You to see

If I'm smiling
Just let me be
This is the
Only way I know
How to cope

It doesn't matter
How I really feel
You have to be kidding
If you think
I'll tell you
The real deal

That would just
Give you the
Opportunity to take
Advantage of me
Or worse yet
Use it against me

I know men
Have done it before
So no more
I'm not taking
Off my layers
Just to be exposed

I'm raw underneath
I can't talk
About it much
I'm scared
He will come back
To take me down
Through the spiral loop
That strips me
Of my hope

It is as if
It is a built in rope
For me to use
To strangle myself
Layer after layer
The twine tightly squeezes
It wraps around my soul
Eliminating what I have
Left of my life

He knows exactly
What to say
And do
To get me back

But I'm smart
I block everyone out
Not allowing anyone
To see the

Layers within me
Sometimes I fear
I may hide them
So well
Even I don't know
How to get in touch
With myself

CHAPTER 5

Throw something
At the wall
Watch it shatter

Hit someone
Knock them to the ground
Watch as they whimper

Answer the door
Watch them search
And question

Man
You've tricked
Them again

CHAPTER 6

Is it melted chocolate
That covers your lips
Or the darkness
Of your soul

You always reassure me
Of course
What I'm thinking
Cannot be true
For I was made for you

Over and over again we dance
And once again
I've given up my stance
For this wonderful thing
Called romance

Your charm holds me captive
As you spin me around and around
But then I feel something round
POUND
POUND
POUND
Somehow I've fallen to the ground

You feel embarrassed
I've said something
That wasn't right

Now your hitting me
With all your might

I hear you yelling
But it sounds
Like I'm underwater
The floor is cold

I sit waiting
To be told
What you really
Think of me

I'm too feeble
To be bold
But then I think
Little does he know
I've been saving dough
Someday I'm planning
To go
Where he'll never find me

I glance out the window
As he walks away
Wondering if I should go today
Yes
Yes
Yes
Today

But then I think
No
I'm not ready today
Anyway
I see he's getting
Better each day

He's putting his
Demons at bay

Today he just had
A bad day
No one's perfect

It's okay
I love him
I say to myself
So
Today I think I'll just stay

Believe

CHAPTER 7

I had to leave
Because
I didn't believe
In myself
Or for that fact
Anyone else

CHAPTER 8

I saw the devil
Yes
I did

He manifested himself
In a man
When he came
To visit the man
I knew it

Vulgar language poured
Out of his mouth
His eyes became
Blanketed with an
Eerie empty stare
Then the physical assaults
Would come
The man would
Bombard me with
His kicking
Punching
Throwing
Slamming

For hours
Sometimes he wouldn't stop
All I could do
Was pray the devil

Would go away
He seemed to
Get a thrill
As I cried
He would scream
At me to
Call on my God

Where is your stupid
God now
He would say
I could only look away

Then I would go
Up above
And just look down
At that pathetic girl
Sitting on the ground
Being beat again
I watched as
She took his sin

The next day
He wondered why
I was so distant

I would just tell him
You hurt me
As he tried to hug me
I pulled away
Now you know
I would never hurt you

That was that
I smiled real big
As I said

I know

You see
I did what
I had to do
To get through

It might seem dumb
That I put up
With him
But the way
I saw it
Was that wasn't
The man I loved
It was the devil
Come to take
His body for a loan

CHAPTER 9

Boom
Like the roaring clap
Of thunder on a humid day
My life is starting
To fade away
Upon closer inspection
I realize this isn't true
For rather I'm beginning anew
Fading fast is my past
More and more
Each day
Leaving me to wonder
Why the hell
Did I stay so long
Crescendos
Signaling major changes
The end has come
From now on
I shall look forward
To those thunderous booms
For they are a reminder
Of the hits that
May have knocked me
Down but now
I'm the one with a pow
My personality is really
Starting to boom loudly

CHAPTER 10

I think about you
A little too often
You seem to soften
In my thoughts
The good memories
Come into my mind
I smile thinking of you

However
The other day
I was at the eye doctor
My headaches have
Been getting worse
I thought it was
My eye prescription
That had to
Be updated
I set up
An appointment to see
What needed to be changed

They sat me in
An exam room
To wait for the doctor
On the wall
Was an eye chart
It got me a bit nervous

I hate it when
The doctor asks me
Better one or better two
Its starts to blur
I cannot tell
They all start to
Look the same

Then I worry
Maybe I told him
The wrong answer
Maybe I saw
Better with one than two
Oh
I don't know

As my eyes darted
Around the room
I saw another chart
This one was
Eye diseases
I should not have looked
Now I think
I'm going blind

Out of the corner
Of my eye
I spied the doctor
Coming my way
He greeted me
Then asked me
What brought me in
I told him

Then he looked at me
And said

Have you ever
Had any head trauma

I stopped thinking
About the eye chart
And the diseases

All of a sudden
I had a flashback
Of you

I was crouched
On the tan carpet
In the corner
You were using
That little metal footstool
Bashing my head

Yes
I said
He used to
Beat me up
Teardrops started to slowly fall
As if they were
Now allowed to finally
Be released

Who would have thought
A trip to the eye doctor
Would bring on
Such a vivid memory
My rose-colored glasses
Don't seem to hide
Your ugliness now
I can see you clearly
Without glasses

CHAPTER 11

He used to tell me
See those homeless people
No one cares about them
Just like no one cares about you
Homeless people die everyday
No one cares
No one investigates
Why they died

Take heed and listen
No one gives a damn
About you
You mean nothing
You are nothing

Don't worry
You'll just disappear
And I won't have a smear
Never fear
They won't think of me
Hah
Hah
Hah
I'm one of them

Don't you get it
I'm the one
With the gun

My bulletproof vest
Makes me one
Of the best
So you can rest
Knowing I'm the
One in charge

As I patrol
The streets at night
I'm keeping the crime
Down on my time

Because it isn't a crime
If no one knows
It happened
And you don't do the time

So think about that
Before you embarrass me
Don't make me
Do something
I might regret

It would be
Your fault
For making me angry
So very irate

I'm never this way
With anyone else
I tell you
You bring out the
Worst in me
See you've done it again

She deserved it

Always getting under my skin
Making me so damn mad
Now she's never going to
Talk back to me again
After all murder isn't a sin

If she made me do it

CHAPTER 12

Salty drops cease tumbling
Down my visage
Serenity forms a bulwark
Surrounding my spirit
Stagnant energy becomes
Kinetic streaming high voltage
Surges through my soul
Directly illuminating my inner self
As if a blinding eclipse
Has taken over
Yet it is only by looking
Directly into the sun
That I have begun
To truly be able to
See who I am

CHAPTER 13

Could it be
That I have
Value that goes
Beyond what I
See in the mirror

I'm questioning
My self -perception
Maybe
He didn't take
Away my worth
Maybe no one can

As I look back
On this special day
When I first
Saw a ray of hope
It was like a lifeguard
Had thrown me a life preserver
Into my sea of troubles

That same rope that
I carried around
All the time dragging
On the ground
Used to be holding me down
But now it was
Going to save me

Cause someone looking
At me in the mirror
Told me I am valuable

CHAPTER 14

Like the bitter pith
Of the sweet orange
This segment of my life
Is bitter at first
For a brief moment

That is until the
Sweet juice squirts
Into my mouth
I taste it
But it lasts only
A moment

Until I crunch down
On a hard seed
Reality is like this
Hard
And
Disgusting

As it reminds
Me of the love
That didn't really love me
Of all the pain
But then I realize
A seed is
What is planted
To grow

Something new
I pause
Yes
I think I'll
Give hope and love
Another chance
Right then they begin
To grow

Then all of a sudden
The painful memories
Come back
With a sheer vengeance
As the tears begin
Flooding my ability
To enjoy life
I am almost ready
To give up

Yet somehow
I manage to
Section that season
Off my life
To be able
To once again
Enjoy life

It's as if the citrus sweetness
Has hit my taste buds
At the right time
Bursting with soft
Deliciousness
For the peeling back
Of the skin
Has rewarded me
With a succulent orange

Suddenly forgotten are
All the work peeling
And the acidic juice
That stung my eyes
The past is over

Or is it
All I can
Taste now
Is the moment
I am in

And it is good

CHAPTER 15

Looking back I see
What you did to me

He's a diamond in the rough
Everything he does
Is more than enough
To make me the happiest girl

Whirl
Whirl
Whirl
Around
And
Around

You were nothing
Like I made you sound
Once you left town
Your lies started falling down
Like pieces of a ripped wedding gown
Your broken pieces of truth
Were nothing but a poof
A poof of air

But you don't seem
To care
It's all gone
Except for some reason

You keep trying
To go on
Don't you realize
It's a throne of lies
You sit upon

If you wake up
You might just see
The gig is up
Yup
That's right
I've regained my sight
Clearly
I can see what you were doing to me
The joke is no longer on me
I've got the key
I'm free
You can no longer manipulate me

CHAPTER 16

Said you knew I was okay
Even though we
Hadn't spoken in a while
Cause you saw me
Flashing a big smile
On my social media

I sadly grinned
On the other end of the phone
That's my imaginary life
It's easy to lie
About my state

All it takes is a fake
That's simple to take
Flash
Flash
Flash
There now I'm happy
Or so you think

See it's all for the likes
I'm pushing a hundred
Then I'll be well liked
It's all on my phone

Funny thing is
My phone never rings

When I'm at home
I sit by myself

Snapping away
Then posting more
And more each day
It's the way
I stay within
Everyone's reach
Or so they think
They don't know

I'm really alone
Hoping to find
A real friend
To spend my time with
One that I can talk to
Without fear that they'll
Run once they see
The real me

CHAPTER 17

Maybe it's no
Big deal to you
But that's not
How I feel
For when I see
An inky smile
Looking at me
I get quite a thrill
You see
My mind gets stuck on
That non-stop reel
Of him
That keeps telling me
I am nothing
I'm stupid
And ugly
A girl who
Will never amount
To anything real
Round
And
Round
That wheel of thoughts
Goes in my head
Especially right before
I go to bed
But not on the nights
I go to class

And see that
Ball point grin
My damaged internal smile
Begins to heal
As his voice becomes
Fainter
And
Fainter
Until I can hardly
Hear his verbal daggers
You see
You are helping
Me silence
His voice
As you make
The choice
To draw
A smiley face
On my paper

Love

CHAPTER 18

Cowering in the corner
That's all you can do
You worthless whore
Pitiful fat pig
Hopeless excuse for a woman
No one else would
Love such an ugly mess
But me

You are lucky
To have me
Love you

Go ahead
Leave me
You'll be back
You'll see
You cannot do it
Not without me

I gave you everything
Life is pretty hard
Out there with no one
To take care of you
Like I do

Don't be stupid

Look at yourself
You don't even have
Any money
Here take a few dollars
See where that
Will get you
Nowhere

Now settle down
Squash your
Crazy ideas

Have a drink
I'm sure you'll see
In the morning
Things will look different

You really don't
Want to leave tonight
It's not safe

I don't want
To have to
Come rescue you
From the bad guys out there

Stop being foolish
You know I'm
Under a bit of stress
It's been a lot lately

Here's your teddy bear
Now sit down
In your favorite chair
We'll watch those
Old movies that you enjoy

And cuddle like
We used to

I'll make some popcorn
And pour you
Another drink

If you want
We can make
Plans to go
To the zoo tomorrow
I promise we
Will go
Not like last time
When I said
We would and never did

Now just stop
All this nonsense

Let's not harp
Over the past

Here pick a movie
Now isn't this
Better than being
On the street
Without me
You could never
Leave me
I know you
You'd miss me
Too much

Who else knows
Everything about you

And how to make
You smile
No one
Right

Now come here
I'll hold you
Tight all night

In the light
Things will look
Different
You will see
Just how much
You love me
Which is why you
Will never leave me

CHAPTER 19

It's just me
Myself
And I
I laugh
To cover up
The fear
Of being by myself

It's scary
As I climb
Up on the counter
To dust a shelf
No one would
Know if I fell
How long would
I be on the ground
Before I would
Be found

A single girl
Can't think too
Long on these
Scenarios
For if she did
The dust
Would kill her
If the fall didn't

I lift my fork
To my lips
Pausing for a moment
Wanting to chat

A little about
My day
And a few more things
I'd like to say

But alas
It's just me
Alone on my chair
Talking to the air

Nights seems so lonely
As I snuggle
Under my comforter
For my bed is
Too big for one
I'm the only one

But then I remember
How bad it was
With the wrong one
How he used to throw
Me to the ground
Stomping on me
Telling me I was worthless

As I ponder
This thought
I think
You're alright
Things are going
To be okay

Just learn to be
Who you were
Created to be
Enjoy this time
As you find out
Who you really are

Value

CHAPTER 20

When I look at him
I think
Wondering what he
Would say
If he knew
Everything
Yes
All the dirt
All the grime
All the choices
I've made

Would he still
Wink at me
When I walked
Past his table
Or would he whisper
Behind my back

What makes me valuable
I'm clueless
All I see
Is the girl
Full of past ghosts
Haunting her
Never letting her
Live outside
Their realm

For if she tries
They whisper
In the wind
You'd never be
The kind of girl
He would want

Come back to us
Where you belong
Do you want
Him to find out
About the real you
He'll reject you
Telling you
You're nothing totally worthless
Just like the others did

It doesn't matter
If you think
You've changed
You'll never find
A man to treat
You like you want
That's not for
Girls like you

Deep down inside you
Is your past
You try to
Push it down
At any second
It might pop out
After all aren't
You comfortable there

You don't know
How to deal
With the things
Of today

It's easier if
You just stay put
In the past
You can't cover up
The things that
Happened to you
Those are a
Part of you

Face it
You are worthless
As you try to work
On yourself
Your head just screams
Don't bother your dirt
It won't work
No one will
Ever love you
Why would they
Even you don't
Love you

Trust never was
Something you could comprehend
Maybe you should give up
Jump off a bridge
Why can't you
Be one of those
Innocent bystanders killed
In a random accident

Then he would
Find out you secret
Everyone would
Find out that
You had been raped

It would be out there
For all to see
After you were dead

So you see
It's no use
Trying to run
From him
You just deserve
More abuse

CHAPTER 21

Do you ever wish
Your life could
Be like a pencil

Where every time
You made a mistake
All it would take
Would be a flip
And a vigorous rub
To erase it
All away

If you wanted
To hone something
All you would
Have to do
Is find a
Good sharpener

That would take
Away the old
Making you new
With just a few
Twists and turns
Your point would
Be ready to write

Then your life

Would be easier
Or would it

All our mistakes
Gone just like that
We couldn't learn
From them
Not all mistakes
Are bad
But we don't
Always see that
Right away

Sometimes we understand
Along the way
That something had
To go wrong
For us to enjoy
The right way

As for the new face
Sometimes I like my
Familiar face staring
Back at me
I like being a little older
If I were a pencil
I would get a new look
Every time I became dull

Afterall if life
Was like a pencil
We'd all shrink
Our erasers before
Our pencil because
Everyone knows your
Eraser always goes

Before your pencil
Is done
Then we would be stuck
With the same old stick
And no eraser

So for today
I think
I'll remain a
Human being
If you know
What I mean

CHAPTER 22

Finally you left him
It took you
A long enough time
To make up your mind

I let that statement go
For I know
They wouldn't understand
The cage that
I was in

From the outside
It was invisible
But to me it was
So very visible

Every day he reinforced
Those bars that
Locked me in
His fist pounded
The nails
Of the words
That caged me in

Soon it was
Impossible for me
To leave him
I was forced

To stay surrounded
By his demons
Who so closely guarded
Me from within
My soul was tired
Of the pain

When would his
Evil reign come
To an end

One day he
Went too far
It gave me
The courage to
Bend the cage bars
That metal wasn't
Easily bent
For he had
Meant it to
Last forever

When I stepped out
Into the world
Where he wasn't
I didn't know
What to do

It felt so unreal
As if it was
Some game he was
Playing on me
Where he would
Pop out of nowhere
Laughing as he
Said

Ha
Ha
Your freedom
Was a joke
The times up

What are you doing
Wondering around
You don't know how
To do anything yourself
It's no use trying
You'll end up dying
Without me in your life

Then he would drag
Me back to
Where I belonged
Day after day
After my escape
That is what I feared

But then one day
He came
It wasn't at all
Like I thought
It would be

He crossed my path
Yes this was my path
He was on
Somehow his words
Seemed like butterflies
In the wind
They didn't affect
Me like they
Used to

Now it was
His turn to wonder
What I was thinking
Why I had a smile

I could see the
Confusion on his face
He couldn't control me
What was this about
Why didn't I just
Follow him to his place
Ignoring his words
I turned to walk away

As I did
I realized I never
Had to go back
To his dangerous place
I had broken free
Now it was
Up to me
To make my
Own safe space
That would put a smile on my face

CHAPTER 23

I rest my head peacefully
Upon my fluffy feather pillow
Then I hear the jingle of his keys
As if the collars of Santa's reindeers
Were jingling to warn me of his arrival

Silence
Boots walking on the tile floor
The usual routine
SNAP
FIZZ
A carbonated beverage opened
Silence
Broken by his boots
Smashing the carpet fibers down
Smothering them with each step
Getting closer and closer

A hand grabs my shirt
Yanking my upper body
Away from my fluffy feather pillow

A mouth yelling obscenities at me
Two arms swinging a metal footstool
Towards my head

WHACK
WHACK

WHACK

Bracing myself against
The white wall
Already full of holes
Revealing the underlying drywall

Status quo

Right

Another night
Another hole in the wall

CHAPTER 24

When I first met him
He impressed me
The way he could
Hold my attention
Won over my affection

It wasn't long
Before I was
Completely enamored
By him
Soon I moved in

Everything was perfect
Until one day
He didn't like
What I said
It was then that I started
To be quite clumsy

That day I tripped
And fell on a hammer
It was pretty obvious
From my eyes
That were black and blue
I needed to be more careful
And watch where I walked

He felt bad

That I looked like a wreck
He went out and brought
Me back an angel food cake
With strawberries
Covered in whipped cream
And my favorite flowers

It made me smile
Shucks
Anyone can trip
Over a hammer
I know he loves me

That fall I started school
He thought it was great
That I was getting out
Into the world
Not to worry
If you don't do well
Good for you for trying

My first grades came in
Much to my surprise
They were all A's
I rushed home
Eager to show him
I'll never forget
He wasn't happy

I tripped again
This time over a caulk gun
It happened to be
Right before my finals
I missed them
He told me see
I think this seals the deal

You aren't meant
To do such things
Why don't you
Put away that dream
It isn't healthy
See how flustered
You are becoming

At test time
Look at you
Your anxiety is high
When you get this way
I don't like it
Calm down
Let me give you a hug
I'll make everything better

Later that month
He popped the question
It was so romantic
On the steps of
The Lincoln Memorial
How could I not say
Yes

All I could see
Were the sparkles
That came off
My new diamond ring
But soon they
Turned to stars
As I tripped again
This time on a paint brush

Now you know
We are going to see

My parents tonight
I expect you to
Smile really big
To let them see
How special you are to me

Here look I even bought
You a new red coat
Now I can't lose
My girl anywhere
You'll be the bell
Of them all
Wearing the red jacket
That separates you from all the others

At his parent's house
Over homemade lasagna
We chatted about colors
Favors and parties
It was all so exciting
I couldn't wait
To be a Mrs.
He seemed happy
That I would be all his
Someday soon
It was all so dreamy

The next day
We met up with his friends
Clumsy me came home
That night and
Tripped again
This time on a chisel
He was quite upset
I wasn't shaping
Into the girl he

Wanted me to be

It made sense
I didn't want to let
My future husband down
Afterall I wanted him
To be happy with me
He deserved to be happy
I secretly resolved
That from now on I would
Give him what
He needed from me

For a little while
This worked well
He thought I was swell

Then strangely enough
I tripped again
This time on a drill
His eyes seemed
To be empty dark holes
As he told me he was
Disappointed in me
I embarrassed him
Now he would
Have to repair
What I broke

I was at a loss
He might leave me
It meant we might not
Ever say I do
No I couldn't live
Without him
He always knew

What to do
Unlike me
Who had no clue
Profusely I apologized to him
Please don't end this
I love you

Turns out he didn't mean it
He just had a bad day
Everything was okay

I was floating
On love's puffy clouds
Happy as could be
That soon he
Would be one with me

But that night
I tripped again
This time it
Was a file
He said we just needed
To smooth a
Few rough edges
Then we'd have
The perfect relationship

Let's kiss and
Forget all this nonsense
I think your favorite movie
Is about ready to start
You take a break
Sit down
Prop your feet up
I'll make the popcorn

A week later
He was mad at me
I don't even know why
Which made me
Trip again
This time it was
On the swiss army knife

Unlike the other falls
He was nowhere near
No
This one I was
Making a choice
To end it all

I couldn't see
Any other way
I wanted to
Finish the job
To cut myself
Out of life

As I sliced my wrist
All I could think
Of was how I
Was letting him down

Soon I was dizzy
Then it got blurry
Lots of people
Gathered around me
Trying to hurry
As they wrapped
My body in white gauze

Then carried me
Out the door
Under the thresh hold
Covered with mistletoe

He didn't follow
The metal box
With red lights
And loud sirens
That held me
Wrapped in white

Could it be
Maybe he
Didn't really love me

CHAPTER 25

Today I am
A superhero
There's nothing
I can't do
Once my yellow
Silky cape is
Draped around my shoulders

Its special powers
Make me bite
Into my statistics
Crunching the numbers
Like a shark
In a tank
With freshly killed fish
I devour my homework
Leaving nothing but
A trail of crumpled
Up scrap paper
And pink eraser remains

With the mask
I can see
What I have within me
The fear is gone
I can do anything

For tonight

I'm learning to fight
For a life
That I will love
One filled with
Restoration
Joy
Empowerment
And
Grace
The mask's holes
Have helped me see
That its more
Than just stats
I'm good at

Maybe I should
Put my cape
On more often
Take it out
Of the box
Instead of sitting around
In my socks

As I look back
I realize that
I was a superhero
In training all along
Now it is time for me
To step into
My destiny
Its okay if I need
A little yellow cape
And a black mask
To help me
See what was
In my soul

All along

CHAPTER 26

Big raindrops hit
My windshield
As I drove past
A neighborhood that
Was less than pristine
Sheets were hanging
In the windows
Behind the crooked
Blind slats
Dirt instead of flowers
Led up to the front doors
It all looked so bleak

Then all of a sudden
I saw a streak
A white puff
Run across the street
In slow motion
His little body
Hit the dark wet street
With a slam
After the SUV
Ran over it

I watched in horror
As the little
Guy just flopped
Onto the ground

The SUV didn't stay
It drove away

I hit my brakes
Hard as could be
Put my car in park

And ran out
To the little white dog
He was in pain
The poor tiny thing
He was yelping
I leaned down
To pick up the
Injured little furbaby
I could tell
By his smell
That he had a dirty life
His fur was matted
He was not
From a happy home
He wasn't loved

I snuggled him stink
And all
As big tears
Rolled down my face
Onto his fur
As if to clean
His tiny shaking body

I didn't know what
I should do
Some of the people
Nearby came out
Of their houses

They yelled at me
What have you done
Killing that dog
But I just stood there
Shaking my head

I didn't kill
This little angel
I only wanted
To save him

He was a little
Piece of heaven
That went back
Where he belonged

As I held him
I'll never forget
His little eyes
They seemed to say
I waited just for
This day when
Someone like you
Would love me
This way even
If just for a moment

I cried even harder
As I knew
What he felt
As I stood
All alone in the
Middle of the road

CHAPTER 27

He looked so peaceful
Sleeping in our bed
I picked up his gun
Damn it was heavy
He wears this
All day
It was loaded

I pointed it at him
Then at myself
If I shot him
What good would
That do me
What if I failed
Like I did
At everything else

I felt the metal
In my mouth
I didn't have any clue
How to be sure
I didn't miss
Knowing my luck
I'll end up
Being an invalid
I wanted everything
To end
Not to go on

Forever in slow motion
Taking the gun
Out of my mouth
I knew I had
To find a way
To never see
Another day

I was done
Glancing at the bed
He was still
Fast asleep

Tiptoeing down the stairs
I thought how to end
The misery I was in
A knife will work
Pulling the handle
Of that kitchen drawer
Seemed to take such force
Then I saw it
The sharp silver blade
It would be
My escape from him
It would be better
Than his gun

As I breathed deeply
I put the sharp tip
Against my wrist
Then I sliced my skin
It didn't hurt
Like I thought it would
It just bled
And bled
I wanted to be dead

This was simple
Just like slicing
A turkey on
Thanksgiving Day

I secretly smiled
This wasn't that hard
Why didn't I do it before
I could have left
A long time ago

I sliced again
Deeper this time
Dark red blood
Began to gush out
All over the floor
But I wanted more
Why was this taking so long

As hard as I could
I sliced deeper into my wrist
Pushing the metal in
My skin split in half
Blood was pouring out

All of a sudden
I felt like I was
Going to die
This was what I wanted
Right
It was happening

I slumped down
On the white kitchen tiles
Which were covered
In a puddle

Of red sin
I thought of all my failures
My family was better
Off without me
He
He was certainly better off

Suddenly for some weird reason
I started getting scared
What if it's all true
And I go to hell
Isn't that where people
Go that end their lives

Things were no longer clear
Now that death
Was near
I was becoming more terrified
With each passing moment

If I could make it
To the phone
Everything was a haze
It seemed like a maze
Just to reach the phone
Across the room

Blood was supposed
To give you life
But not mine
It was just a mess
Proof that my life
Didn't mean a thing
Just something else
That had to be mopped up
After I was gone

He would be mad
If he saw the bloody scene
No I think its best if I go

This is best
I felt like a wheel
Spinning
But getting nowhere
My heart began
To pound
Like a hammer
On a nail
As the nail
That would soon
Seal my coffin

I started to cry
I don't know why
Ending things should have
Made me feel better

I slithered my pathetic
Half corpse of a body
Through the bloody puddles
Leaving a trail that would stain
That white grout
It would never come out

I don't remember much
After I reached the phone
Except the loud
Pound on the door
It must have woken
Him up
He came downstairs

In a sleepy state
He looked at me
Repulsed by what
He saw
He looked away
That was all
He had to say
Without a word
He let me know

Walkie talkie radios
Surrounded me
They put me
On a stretcher
No
He didn't want to
Go with me
He didn't care
To see what happened
To me

In the ambulance
Needles and tubes
Poked me
This way and that
These people kept
Telling me that
I have so much to live for
But they didn't understand
I had nothing to live for
I really did want to die
I didn't want to hold on

Or at least I thought so
Turns out that
My death wish

Did not come true
My guardian angel

Was on overtime
That night

And those people
In the ambulance
They were right
I really do have so
Much to live for
Now that he
Is no longer
A part of my life

CHAPTER 28

As I signed up
For a bag of food
Poverty's shame reared
Its ugly head
Telling me what
A loser I was
How I had stooped
So low as to
Ask for food

That condescending voice
Told me I was nothing
I deserved nothing
It tried to prevent me
From picking up
That bag of food
I desperately needed
It said that
If I had
Never left him
Things wouldn't have
Gotten this bad

I looked at my shoes
As I walked toward
The building
I almost turned back
But I didn't

I rang the bell
That let me know
I was safe here
He couldn't hurt
Me anymore

I was learning
How to do things
Yes
It was a struggle
But I was
Not going
To be in
Poverty forever

I took a deep breath
Then walked in
What happened next
Wasn't what I had
Expected would be
For they were delighted
That I was there
I blinked twice
These ladies were so nice
They looked at me
With tender compassion
I was overwhelmed
With gratitude

For the first time
In a long time
I felt wanted
I felt loved

They smiled softly
Then brought me

A big brown bag
Filled with food
And a gift card

I felt special
I felt like I mattered

It was three days
Before Thanksgiving Day
But I was ever so thankful
For those two lovely angels
They never judged me
Their tenderhearted eyes
Were filled with kindness
They made me feel
Like a human
I don't think they
Will ever know
Just how special
They made me feel

What they gave me
Was more than food
It was the blessing of
Love and self-dignity
Concepts which are
Hard for me to accept

I smiled the
Whole way home

Upon opening my bag
A tear slid
Down my cheek
Someone really cared
About me

They cared enough
To neatly pack
My bag with

The cans and the boxes
All turned the right way
While managing to
Maneuver a turkey pan
Into the package

What really impacted me
About the bag
Was not one of the
Cans were dented
Nor were any boxes
Crushed or ripped

I paused to ponder this

Could it be
That I have
Value that goes
Beyond the image
I see of myself
It caused me
To question
My self-perception

Someone had taken
The time to pack
My bag in such
A manner that nothing
Was damaged

Is it time
For me to

Follow their example
And repack my bags
With dent free cans
And undamaged boxes

I'm beginning to think so.

CHAPTER 29

I didn't need any help
Everything was fine
But I knew
I could not go on
Like this forever
One day it would end

I was making a plan
It was going
To happen on my timetable
I was saving money
Making sure I
Would be okay

I could put up
With him for
As long as I needed
Or so I thought

One day by accident
He dialed my friend
Who heard the devil
That he pretended
Not to be
She called the police

He innocently answered
The door

He looked at them
Baffled as to why
They were at our love nest
We are in love
Look at my lovely fiancé

In fact if you'll excuse me
I must hurry
Our brunch reservations
Are soon
Why yes
You've been there
It's one of our favorites
Thank you for your service
To the community
It's great to know
The men in blue
Are keeping us safe

Come on sweetheart
Let's go

Off we went
Never to mention
Anything of the reality
Of what had happened
Earlier that day

What he didn't know
Nor did I
Was who called the police
But I think he
Noted to himself
To be a bit more
Of a sneak

Later that day
My friend called
She wanted to know
If I was okay

Of course
I was
I said
He was sitting
Right beside me
We're in the middle of brunch

That's good
She replied
Let's grab a drink
Tomorrow night
Sounds like a plan
If we include a bite

The next evening
A few drinks in
She paused
Then told me
She was terrified
Of what she had heard
I didn't know
What she meant
Then she proceeded
To tell me
About the phone call
Which evidently no one
Knew about
Not knowing what
To do
She called the police

I nodded
It all made sense now
I was so embarrassed
My secret was out

All she said to me
That night was
Anytime
Anytime
Anytime
Call day or night
You are welcome
Anytime
Anytime
Anytime
What about your husband
He knows
Anytime
Anytime
Anytime
I teared up

It would take me
Quite sometime after
Her offer to accept it

But one night
The devil came out again
He didn't have
The chance to beat me
For I knew
When I smelled
The smoke of
His pitchfork he
Was ready to poke

Not this time
You can't have my soul
I have a way out
It was midnight
She answered
Like she said
She would
Anytime
Anytime
Anytime

CHAPTER 30

Why be frightened
Of something that is
Not real
And only once a year
Halloween
It's all fake fear
As the lights flicker
And grave diggers dance
With tasty treats
All ghoulishly good
As screams of terror
Are heard on rides
In the dark

Did I hear this right
Someone wants to be
Scared at night
Well my friend
Look no further
I will tell you my story

I deal with being scared
Every day of the year
As he screams
In my ear
Telling me that
I am nothing
I should

Be ever so lucky
That he loves me

Tears used to fall
From my face
Now I just disappear
In my head
To a different place
One that's safe
I dream of puppy dogs
Of princes that come
From kissing frogs

But then I must
Snap out of it
As his fist punches my lip
A little blood
Runs down my chin
Like a vampire
Now he's sucking
The life out of me
Role reversal I think they say

I pull away
Why does life
Have to be this way
He stops

This time it wasn't too bad
Or so that's what
I tell myself
It's only a busted lip
I can cover it up

Don't you know
My costume is the best

I cover my body
From head to toe
For you will never know
How many blows
Only that I am okay

Because I know
How the wear the mask
And the whole costume
Just perfectly

It hides all the pain
Don't you dare
Try to take it
Off of me
For if you do
I may have to say
Boo
Then you may
Be really scared
Of the real me
The one that lets
Him beat me
He laughs and says
You're crazy
For no one
Will ever believe you
You stayed with me
All this time
You are all mine
Shhhhhhhh

This is part of the mask
I wear it with a secret
The terror inside
Cannot be let out

For if it was
People would find
Out the truth
And I would be to blame

Why didn't you just leave
They would say

I would look
The other way
Wishing I had my mask
But it doesn't work
That way
Once the mask is off
I'm raw

Maybe you are wondering
Why I took
Off my mask

Because it was time
To live again
Breathing air not constricted
By his cruel words
That seemed to strike me
Harder than any
Of his blows
To dance again
Moving freely
No longer bound
By his manipulating hands
That used to leave
Tattoos of him
All over me
Taunting me telling me
As I looked at myself

You'll never leave
You can't leave
He's marked you
For good
Who would want you

But I left

Now I'm naked
As I stand here
With no mask
Or costume to hide
The real me
In front of you
Looking around
Wondering how many more
Of you are hiding
Under your masks
Or costumes of
Clearly I'm doing fine

Won't you take them off
Like me
Stand up here with me
Together we can
Let the world know
It's time to take
Off our masks
To live in freedom
Without abuse

About the Author

Christine is a survivor of domestic abuse, rape and sex trafficking. She recently found poetry to be an excellent outlet for her to convey her experiences in a manner that is ambiguous enough to help other survivors. Christine is working on another book of poetry about rape and PTSD. She hopes to be able to open the dialog for issues that constantly keep survivors in the victim state as they usually are too ashamed to share their stories. As a survivor, the power is within you to make a difference in the world. You survived for a reason. Don't let that reason go to waste. Stand up and take your God-given power back!